PLEIADES ART BOOKS

GENERAL EDITOR: JAMES LAVER

TWENTIETH CENTURY
SCULPTURE

BY THE SAME AUTHOR:

AN INTRODUCTION TO MODERN ART

TWENTIETH CENTURY SCULPTURE

E. H. RAMSDEN

LONDON : PLEIADES BOOKS : MCMXLIX

FIRST PUBLISHED 1949
BY PLEIADES BOOKS LTD 11 FITZROY SQUARE LONDON W1
PRINTED IN GREAT BRITAIN
BY THE SHENVAL PRESS LONDON AND HERTFORD

PREFACE

Owing to the many difficulties which still beset the path of the scholar as a result of the war, the review of the sculpture of this century which is here presented is, as I am only too well aware, neither so comprehensive nor so complete as I should like to have made it.

I hope, however, that notwithstanding the limits which circumstances have imposed upon me I have been able to indicate at least the main trends of sculptural development in recent times. Not every country in Europe has been represented and not every sculptor who might have been included in a wider survey, while the work of those who are unwilling to take part in 'collective manifestations' has necessarily had to be omitted.

The arrangement of the material has been conditioned by the plates at my disposal which I found could best be grouped in an alphabetical order of countries, an exception being made only in the case of England, whose contribution I have discussed first and, for obvious reasons, rather less briefly than that of the others. This, I hope, has not upset the balance of the book.

In conclusion I should like to thank those artists and others who, by their prompt and considerate replies to letters, did much to ease the performance of a task that could not have been accomplished without the kind assistance of members of the staff of the Victoria & Albert Museum and the Tate Gallery, of the Directors of museums and galleries abroad and of Mrs Mendelssohn Bartholdy, Miss Erica Brausen, Mr Douglas Cooper, Dr Paul Hodin, Dr Kihlbom, Mr Frank McEwan, Mr George L. K. Morris, Miss Greta Ring, Signor Orlando Ruggiero, Señor Pi Sunyer and Mr Curt Valentin, to all of whom I am exceedingly grateful. In addition, I should like to thank Mr Meyrick R. Roger for permission to reproduce his photograph of the *Sun Singer* by Carl Milles; Mr E. C. Gregory, Messrs Arthur Tooth & Sons and Mr A. Zwemmer for having afforded facilities for the photographing of sculpture in their collections; the Editor of the *Museums Journal* for the loan of the block of *Sibelius* by Wäinö Aaltonen, and Margot Eates for her untiring help with the Index.

CHELSEA   E. H. RAMSDEN

June 1948

5

CONTENTS

LIST OF PLATES

1

ERIC GILL: Crucifixion. *Hoptonwood Stone.* 1910

Tate Gallery, London. *Photo: Roland Federn,* A.R.P.S.

2

ERIC GILL: Flying Angel. *Portland Stone.* c.1928

Victoria & Albert Museum, London

3

JOHN SKEAPING: Pouter Pigeon. *Alabaster.* c.1933

Arthur Tooth & Sons. *Photo: Paul Laib*

4

RICHARD BEDFORD: Opening Bud. *Roman Stone.* 1940

Artist's possession

5

JACOB EPSTEIN: Rabindranath Tagore. *Bronze.* 1927

Birmingham Art Gallery. *Photo: Paul Laib*

6

FRANK DOBSON: Sir Osbert Sitwell. *Polished Brass.* 1923

Tate Gallery, London (loan)

7

HENRY MOORE: Mother and Child. *Burgundy Stone.* 1931

Collection: Miss MacCaw. *Photo: E. J. Mason*

8

HENRY MOORE: Reclining Figure. *Elm Wood.* 1940

Collection: Miss Elizabeth Onslow-Ford

9

BARBARA HEPWORTH: Pierced Hemisphere. *White Marble.* 1937

Wakefield Art Gallery

10

BARBARA HEPWORTH: Elegy. *Beech Wood.* 1946

Collection: Mrs S. Kaye

11

ROBERT ADAMS: Seated Woman. *White Marble.* 1947

Artist's possession

12

F. E. MCWILLIAM: Reclining Woman. *Terra-cotta.* 1947

Artist's possession

7

9

TWENTIETH CENTURY SCULPTURE

Broadly speaking the history of sculpture in Europe follows the same lines and conforms to the same pattern in every country.

Towards the end of the nineteenth century the standard of achievement generally had reached so low a level that, had it not been for the emergence of one or two sculptors of outstanding genius, sculpture might well have ceased to belong to the category of the fine arts and might, as a decorative art, have become, to an even greater degree than it has, increasingly ornamental and decreasingly artistic in an age like our own, in which culture has become a hybrid and taste is unknown.

Because it is in some respects a more limited art than painting, sculpture has tended not only to remain bound by the traditions of the past, but also to repeat the same formulas continually and with little variation, save that which is incidental to its period. Also, because virtuosity is more common than genius, the attempts which have frequently been made to offset the difficulties inherent in its practice by men of lesser attainments have more often than not resulted in the production of work which, though it may astound the vulgar, is hardly likely to deceive the *élite*.

Of the three main styles in sculpture, the classical, the gothic and the baroque, the classical has predominated; partly because it was, at least in so far as Europe is concerned, in the classical mode that sculpture, the art *par excellence* of the Greeks, received its definitive form, 'every product of the waking consciousness of the Classical world', as Spengler has said, being 'elevated to the rank of actuality by way of sculptural definition', and partly, because it was in this mode that the study of the nude, a study beloved of sculptors of all climates and ages, was most naturally developed. In addition, the revival of the antique during the Renaissance promoted in sculpture a taste for heroic and mythological themes that has persisted down to the present day.

A conspicuous instance of this tendency to regard the manner of the ancients as the manner to which above all sculpture should aspire is seen, for example, in the art of the Danish sculptor, Thorwaldsen, which, except that it is free from the histrionics by which so much of the art of the period was vitiated, leaves, in spite of its Praxitelean perfection (or perhaps because of it), almost everything to be desired.

In nearly every country from Norway to Portugal the reaction against this pseudo-classicism, which inevitably set in, found expression in a type of realism that is intrinsically so little suited to sculpture that it amounts almost to an anomaly. But that it is in some instances an expression of genuine feeling is exemplified in the work of the Belgian sculptor, Constantin Meunier, whose realistic figures of the working man date only from the time of his visit to the Black Country, where, as he said, 'the creative work of my life was revealed to me'.

A less successful example of realism in sculpture than Meunier's *Puddler* or *Miner* has been provided in our own time in Sargeant Jagger's bronze figures on the *Artillery Memorial* at Hyde Park Corner, which whatever else they may not be are certainly a triumph for the founder. And that they are not more than this arises from the fact that an excessive pre-occupation with extraneous detail on this scale (or on any other, for that matter) must necessarily divert the artist and prevent him from realizing those ends for which art exists and in the attainment of which alone his efforts are justified.

The introduction of a wealth of irrelevancies, however dexterously these may be handled, is therefore no compensation for a lack of the true incentive; yet it is owing to the assumption on the part of the schools that this kind of facility is a good instead of a bad second, that the term 'academic', when it is used in relation to art, has acquired its pejorative connotation, implying, as it does, work that is technically competent but artistically inept.

What, for instance, can be said in defence of Sir William Reid Dick's *Memorial Statue of George V*, which, beyond being a tolerable likeness, is as artistically unredeemed as it is intrinsically unworthy of the great King whose life of service to his people it is designed to commemorate. It has not even the quiet dignity of the *Kitchener Memorial* in St Paul's Cathedral, which, though it is not great sculpture, seems by comparison unimpeachable. Set at a height at which it can only be seen in perspective at an unsafe distance (i.e. in the middle of the road), the figure, which has only one leg and is both anatomically and sartorially faulty below the waist, is hopelessly dwarfed by the theatrical management of the robes and by the clumsy handling of the accessories. To treat a statue of this kind naturalistically (as it should be) is one thing, to treat it stylistically (as it might be) is also one thing, but to treat it in a fashion that is at once neither and both is wholly and patently inadmissible. On technical grounds the work, as in so many academic productions, is further invalidated by the total lack of a sense of material which it displays. For there can, in fact, be no creative use of stone in work that is pointed up by a technician from a clay model and may not even be finished by the artist. It is true, of course, that much of Rodin's work, which originated in clay, was pointed up in his studio in this way, but then Rodin, after all, was Rodin, just as Diaghilev was Diaghilev—'Stop eating peas off a knife,' said he to a ballerina. 'But you eat peas off a knife!' 'That is a different matter, I am Diaghilev.'

Although sculpture is not an art in which to say nothing with all the verbosity of a twentieth-century demagogue, it is prone either to degenerate into the banalities of an artificial and outworn symbolism, or else to imitate nature in so slavish a fashion that it becomes artistically meaningless, since there is a degree of verisimilitude and of mechanical perfection beyond which art cannot go. So that had it not been for the inspiration of those men for whom art was something more than an imitation or a pastiche, the stultification of the creative impulse at this stage would have been complete. It is, therefore, obvious that towards the end of the nineteenth century a break with the conventional aims and methods of the past had become imperative. Moreover, the agnosticism of the period was, in itself, sufficient to bring all other values into question, while its scientific developments, which are marked in painting in the new worlds of artistic possibility which were revealed as a result of Chevreul's analysis of colour, inevitably led to changes more radical than any that had before taken place, not only in art, but in every other field of cultural activity.

In art this repudiation of the conventions of the past was manifested in two ways. It was signalized, first of all, in the evolution of impressionism, in which all the hitherto accepted rules of painting were transgressed in the interests of a more vital mode of expression; and later in the cult of the primitive, in which the desire of an effete generation to regain something of that vigour and spontaneity which belongs to the work of an earlier age is unequivocally announced.

14

Sculpture, being a three-dimensional and therefore a more severely conditioned art than painting, shows, however, a less violent reaction against traditional practices. Yet, while it lends itself less naturally to an impressionistic treatment, it gained in the hands of Medardo Rosso and Auguste Rodin a new power of emotional expression, just because it did not accord with those ideals of plastic beauty which had formerly been regarded as absolute. But if on technical grounds it does not conform to the standards of pure sculpture, it is nevertheless justified, inasmuch as the ruggedness of the form is perfectly suited to the romantic nature of the content, in addition to which the very reaction against the pseudo-classical style which it symbolized led in turn to a reassertion of those formal principles, which, though they remain ultimate, can only be recognized as such to the extent to which they are continually revitalized and reinterpreted in terms of the contemporary ideal to which they are related. For whatever innovations may be made there is not, and happily never can be, a complete severance of the past from the present, since, through the involution and evolution of thought, there must always be a return to first principles in the action, reaction and interaction of ideas. For this reason no phase of artistic development can be finally understood except in relation to that mode which it succeeds. Nor perhaps could there be a greater tribute to Rodin's genius than the force of his influence, on the one hand, and the violence of the reaction against it, on the other. Yet notwithstanding its power, Rodin's art was essentially an individual art, both spiritually and technically, so that it is not surprising that in comparison with the more impersonal achievement of Aristide Maillol, which belongs in principle to the recognized order of sculptural tradition, its influence should have been limited. In fact it is, indisputably, Maillol's influence that has proved to be the most formative in the field of representational art in the present century, not only in France but in other parts of Europe.

To the western mind, with its accumulation of inherited prejudices, African Negro sculpture, which was first exhibited in Paris and later in London before the Great War, came both as a shock and a revelation. Ritualistic in character and having little or nothing to do with the niceties of objective truth, it presented an entirely new world of formal possibilities to painters and sculptors alike. In the first place, it did much through its elimination of non-essentials to stimulate and encourage the revolt of the *avant-garde* against prevailing academic practices, and in the second, by its sheer vitality it gave a fresh impetus to the creative effort of a generation who recognized instinctively that the time for a restatement of artistic premises had come. For just as its discovery coincided stylistically with the evolution of Cubism, which in painting constituted a logical development from Post-Impressionism, so its coming corresponded historically with the beginning of a period of social and political disruption, both national and international, of which the effects today are everywhere manifest.

With its primitive insistence upon those features of the design that are symbolically significant and its virtual denial of those that are not, Negro sculpture, in its uncompromising boldness of purpose, achieves, as far as its formal values are concerned, something of the same effect as that which is produced by Cubism in its simpler resolutions of form into the elementary shapes of the sphere, the cylinder and the cone. But while painting, which is the subtler art by reason of its abstract use of pattern and colour, lent itself to the composing of endless variations on the Cubist theme, sculpture, which is more circumscribed, soon exhausted its immediate possibilities. It is noteworthy, however, that once the focus of interest and attention had shifted from the figurative to the non-figurative, and the measure of the likeness of this or that object to nature no longer constituted a criterion, the advancement from the simplification to the abstraction of form and from the abstraction to the creation of form in an absolute sense was as rapid as it was inevitable. Yet just because of the limitation of its scope in other directions, it is sculpture, as the art of form *par excellence*, which has reached the highest exemplification of the ideals of a non-representational art. Nor was this the case in one school or in one country only. In Switzerland, in Russia, in Italy and in England it was in sculpture that the most notable and impressive experiments were made. Unfortunately, however, some of the most important of this constructive work is very little known, being seldom seen and less often illustrated, which would seem something of an anomaly, considering the professed desire of some of its exponents to get it to 'the masses', not of course that 'the masses' would be in the least impressed by so highly esoteric an art even if it were 'got' to them. 'Home,' said Sir Beerbohm Tree, throwing himself into a hansom. 'And where, sir, *is* your home?' inquired the cabman, after driving round for some time. 'And why,' replied the actor, 'should I tell a common man like you where my beautiful home is?' Ah, why indeed? It is, nevertheless, regrettable that so sensitive and beautiful an achievement and one that is of the greatest aesthetic significance should remain comparatively unknown, more particularly as much of the work is lacking in durability, a virtue which has hitherto been regarded as fundamental to sculpture, being executed, as it is, in plastic materials which science has rendered available, but has not yet proved.

A concern with material is not, however, peculiar to those artists who have employed the less usual materials—metal, perspex, rodoid, etc.—but is characteristic also of those who continue to work in stone and in wood. For no longer does the artist strive to torture his material into the likeness of 'soft flesh', but rather to seek in the nature of his material the elements of the idea which it contains. For, as an old Yorkshireman admiringly exclaimed at the sight of one of Henry Moore's carvings in elm, 'I have been working in wood all my life, but I could not do that!' Hence the paradox—that the modern sculptor is a realist with a difference, since while progressively eliminating all the trappings of a sensible reality, he is yet continually working towards the realization of certain forms which he feels to be ultimate. Similarly, while his work in its architectonic and constructive character clearly reflects the mechanical tendencies of his age, he himself, in his advocacy of a personal craftsmanship, as opposed to the technical practices of the schools, has given proof of his recognition that sculpture no less than painting is primarily an activity of the soul.

Of this fact no artist was more keenly aware than the English sculptor, Eric Gill, who by practice, principle and precept was opposed to everything that the academicians stood for.

In the first place, having been trained as a stonemason and having acquired an early respect for the sound traditions of English craftsmanship, he naturally grew to appreciate the importance of direct carving and the necessity of conceiving a composition in terms of the material in which it is to be executed. Secondly, as a result of his early training, during which his gift for lettering was fostered by his association with the calligrapher, Edward Johnstone, he came to perceive the need for adopting a more austere approach to sculpture and for reintroducing that simplicity of design which is characteristic of the work of the primitives, but is conspicuously lacking in that of later times. It is true that in his endeavour to break away from the artificialities with which public monuments and commemorative sculpture generally had come to be associated, he tended to a use of archaisms that are mannered and self-conscious in another way, yet even so and notwithstanding the personal eccentricities into which it led him, it would be difficult to over-estimate the importance of his teaching. For such was the level of mediocrity to which sculpture had fallen by the end of the last century that it is probable that without the regaining of a primitive vitality and a return to the direct method sculpture as an art would scarcely have survived. It is significant, moreover, that it was at about the same time that the practice of working *en taille directe* was initiated in France under the leadership of Josef Bernard, one of the most sensitive and delightful artists of his period.

Considered independently and without reference either to his Socialism or to his Catholicism, Gill's particular contribution to the art of his time is not entirely to be understood; but when it is seen in relation to his personality and his background, much that at first seems arbitrary is seen to be less affected than it appears. Being a typical product of his *milieu* and having something of the fanaticism of the social reformer and the convert (for it must not be forgotten that Gill and his family lived according to the order of a religious community), he naturally tended to a form of expression that seems peculiar to the layman, accustomed as he is to the more fluent banalities of a drawing-room art. Yet while Gill was mainly attracted to the execution of religious themes, he also produced work of a secular character some of which is frankly grotesque in a curiously repulsive way, being the antithesis of everything that is given in his *St Sebastian*, a carving in Portland stone that has been described as one of the most exquisite of his productions. *The Crucifixion* of 1910, which is now in the Tate Gallery and is typical of Gill at his best, illustrates at once the simplicity of his method and the fineness of his lettering, though the inscription is, in this instance, somewhat obtrusive, as it often is in his *Stations of the Cross*, the more famous carvings in low relief in Westminster Cathedral which he undertook immediately after his conversion to the Roman Church in 1913. In these carvings, as in that of the *Flying Angel* which he executed at the time when he was working on the three *Winds* for the Underground Station at St James's Park, the static character of his conception is evident, for Gill's art is essentially a symbolic art, even when he is concerned with the portrayal of non-religious subjects.

For reasons which are not immediately obvious, it is as carvers rather than as modellers that English sculptors have excelled. It is therefore hardly surprising, despite the popularity of his work, that Rodin has had practically no influence on the development of the younger men in this country, whereas the influence of Negro sculpture has been extensive. Yet while the study of primitive carving has been beneficial in so far as it has promoted an interest in fundamental problems and has given rise to a new phase of sculptural activity, it has been unfavourable to the extent to which it has led to the cultivation of an assumed naïveté and of a deliberate awkwardness of manner that cannot finally be justified. Nevertheless, to accuse an artist like John Skeaping, who was at one time in the forefront of the experimentalists, of a desire to *épater le bourgeois* when he gave himself to the carving of his *Akua-ba*, for instance, would be to misunderstand his motives completely. At the same time, to maintain that he was sincere in his choice of such a form at the time of its execution, a time when he was strongly influenced by his study of primitive types, is not to argue that no other forms of expression were open to him, since he is plainly capable, both as a sculptor and as a draughtsman, of expressing his reactions to life with a clarity that is unquestionable. It is therefore the more to be regretted that he has not fulfilled the exceptional promise which he showed as a young man, owing it would seem rather to a lack of opportunity than to anything else, for he combines at once the instinct of the carver and the naturalist, if one may judge from his *Pouter Pigeon*, which shows at once his understanding of those principles of economy that are fundamental to the art of carving, his appreciation of natural form, and his perception of the need to push its abstraction to the farthest limits of which it is capable. It shows, too, his feeling for material, a feeling which he formerly expressed in the experimental carving of many unusual stones.

This interest in material is shared, also, by Richard Bedford, who probably knows more about technical processes than any other sculptor in the field today. But it is less with glyptic than with abrading methods that he himself is concerned, for which reason it is with the harder marbles and with stones that have not habitually been used by sculptors that he has experimented. But whether in the use of chisels or abrasives, the same need for economy of method persists, though one may well imagine that the temptation to carry a design farther than is necessary is stronger in the use of the first than of the second, especially if a work on the scale of Bedford's *Cat* is considered, a work that is over life-size and is executed in Genoa marble, a green limestone which is exceptionally hard. His *Opening Bud*, on the other hand, which was one of the most popular works shown at the exhibition of contemporary art at the London Museum during the war, is partly abraded and partly carved. Indeed, though it expresses rather less fully than some of his flower motives that 'organization of form symbolic of human-animal-vegetable life' of which Wilenski has spoken in connection with his work, it is perhaps the most satisfactory of his carvings.

Another English artist who is primarily a carver, notwithstanding the fact that he has produced a number of works in bronze, is Frank Dobson, who has not only developed the study of the nude, but has also executed a variety of portrait-busts, in addition to doing such architectural work as the decoration of the façade of Hay's Wharf in a series of reliefs in gilded faience. But if his carvings of seated, standing and reclining female figures are reminiscent of Maillol's treatment of the same subject in their directness of approach and lack of elaboration, they are entirely without that firmness of structure and fineness of modelling by which the work of the French master is distinguished. For this reason Dobson is seen to greater advantage in those examples of his work in which the form is simplified almost to a point of semi-abstraction, as is the case in some of his more recent carvings. As to his portrait-busts, these are interesting in that, whether consciously or not, he tends to adapt his medium and his technique to the character and individual peculiarities of the sitter; in none of them has he done so with greater effect than in his deservedly famous bust of *Sir Osbert Sitwell*, in which the unusual choice of polished brass would seem to accord perfectly with the brilliance and originality of the man whom the work portrays.

With Jacob Epstein, who is of Russian-Polish origin, though he has lived the best part of his life in England, we come to one of the most controversial figures of the century. By some he is decried as an innovator who is concerned only 'to shock and wound the minds of men', while by others he has been commended, together with Meštrović, as one of the only two considerable sculptors in Europe today; but like all exaggerated expressions of opinion they are both wrong, nor would Epstein himself be slower in the denial of the second than of the first.

But while it would clearly be idle to pretend that Epstein has not shocked society by such carvings as *Genesis*, *Adam* and *Behold the Man*, to allege that he did so of set purpose is no more justifiable than to assume that he is insincere in his intentions simply because his carvings have proved repugnant to the generality. On the contrary, he has consistently had the courage of his convictions, for no one can deny the truth of his statement, 'I have, despite every obstacle of organized hostility on the part of the Press, art critics, art cliques and personal vendettas, gone my own way and have never truckled to the demands for popularity.'

It is, however, as a modeller rather than as a carver that he must here be considered, not only because there is no scope in a brief survey of this kind to enter into a discussion of the merits or demerits of work that still remains so debatable a subject, but also because it is in his bronzes that his virtues as a sculptor are finally and unambiguously revealed. And if of these the busts are to be preferred to the full-length figures, it is because they demand a more complete control of that dynamic force by which Epstein is animated, while affording no opportunity for a weakening of the design by peculiarities of gesture that are not inherent in the composition. They give, too, unmistakable proof of the keenness of his observation of character and of his uncompromising translation of the psychological, as of the physical, features of his sitters into plastic terms. Also, because of the vigour of his attack, and because, in male portrait-busts, he tends to be less distracted by irrelevant considerations, he has on the whole been more successful in his rendering of men than of women. For this reason it is in such a bust as that of the Indian poet, *Rabindranath Tagore*, that Epstein is seen at his best, the massive character of the head, which is perfectly set off by the slightness of the curve by which the shoulders are indicated, being eminently suited to Epstein's boldness of technique as a modeller and to his breadth of style as a *busteur*.

Another sculptor who has been particularly successful in the portrayal of Oriental personalities is the Russian-born artist, Dora Gordine, who, having lived and worked in the East, has an intimate understanding of the inwardness of the eastern attitude to life. This she has realized with consummate skill in her head of a *Chinese Philosopher*, while by accentuating the natural compactness of the physical conformation she has succeeded in producing a work that is not only superb as portraiture, but is also sculptural in the highest sense of the word. The head, with its curved surfaces, shows, too, the closeness of her method to that of Maillol, by whom she has been considerably influenced. For Gordine is not exclusively a *busteur*, but has devoted herself with equal energy to the study of the nude. This has for her a quite different interest, however, from what it had for Maillol, despite her liking for rounded and voluptuous forms, since whereas Maillol nearly always modelled his famous *femme Maillol* in positions of repose, Gordine is generally more concerned with the rhythmic flow of the movement through the limbs. She has, accordingly, made a special study of dancers, though less with the intention of rendering the movements of the dance, than of observing the more subtle movements of the body as it turns naturally and with the unconscious grace of a young animal from one position to another.

Unlike the majority of sculptors, Henry Moore has never been the disciple of any 'master', which is perhaps one of the reasons why his work is so eminently individual. This is not, however, to say that there are no influences detectable in his work, since this is manifestly not so, but those that there are, and they are clear and unmistakable, are those of the so-called 'Primitives' whom he studied with enthusiasm when he came to London in 1921 to work at the Royal College of Art, after he had completed his preliminary training at the School of Art in Leeds. And of the primitive influences, it was that of Mexican art, particularly of the Aztec period, which proved decisive in his development as a sculptor. 'As soon as I found it,' he writes, 'it seemed to me good and right, perhaps because I at once hit on the similarities in it with some of the eleventh-century carvings I had seen as a boy on Yorkshire churches.' Thus, from the very beginning, Moore seems to have recognized intuitively what elements were and what were not in accord with the ultimate realization of his genius, and to have followed without any deviation that course which alone seemed consistent with his ideals. For as he said at a later date, 'Beauty in the later Greek or Renaissance sense, is not the aim of my sculpture. Between beauty of expression and power of expression there is a difference of function. The first aims at pleasing the senses, the second has a spiritual vitality, which is for me more moving and goes deeper than the senses.'

Like all modern sculptors who have drawn their inspiration from a study of the primitives, Moore has an intense feeling for material, whether it be for the stoneness of stone, the woodness of wood, the leadness of lead or the concreteness of concrete. 'Seeing, then, that he has the instinct of a master-craftsman, it is without violation of the peculiar properties of his material that Moore has sought the realization of those ideas in which "the abstract principles of design" and "the psychological human element" are combined, it is the more instructive to observe in what way the expression of the idea is conditioned by the material in which it is executed, and, conversely, in what way the choice of the material is determined by the nature of the idea to be expressed. For example, in stone the emphasis

19

is on mass or "block rhythms" with relatively little abstraction; in wood, a more fluent movement supervenes with a greater penetration of the material; in concrete and metal, the emphasis changes from the glyptic to the structural or architectonic, though without loss of tactile effect; while in the string figures, surface unit gives place to a new mode of inter-connectedness with a corresponding increase in tension.'[1]

Yet, while acknowledging the need for abstraction, at least in a degree in all art and more particularly in sculpture in which the nature of the material itself 'forces one away from the pure representational', Moore has never lost sight of the organic principle on which his art is founded. So that to whatever limits he may push an idea in the exploration of its sculptural possibilities, he almost invariably maintains a sense of man's deep and enduring contact with nature, which may be expressed either in terms of man's humanity as man or in terms of man's relationship to the landscape in which he lives. The first is exemplified in his *Mother and Child*, a typical work of his earlier period which illustrates both the generic character of his conception and the direct method of his approach, inasmuch as the subject is treated in a manner which lays no stress upon the individuality of the mother or child, while the carving is reduced to the minimum and is devoid of any kind of elaboration whatsoever. As to the second, this is perfectly shown in the great *Reclining Figure* in elm wood which is eight years later in date. Here the intimate oneness of the life of nature and the life of man is expressed as much by the way in which the bole of the tree is utilized to indicate the form of the figure which emerges from it, as by the feeling of unity which is conveyed by the introduction of the holes by means of which the inward and the outward become, as it were, identified. Yet although the figure is part of the tree and the tree of the landscape, it is not the figure of the dryad of classical myth that Moore has portrayed, but rather that of some primordial goddess who antedates man and to whom, as Galsworthy remarked in another connection, the notion that it is man who is the dominating factor in nature must seem a rather 'parvenu conviction'.

That Moore should have acquired an international reputation in his pursuit of an art which, if it is not exactly 'difficult', is certainly lacking in any kind of popular appeal, is due perhaps as much to his complete consistency as an artist as to his indisputable genius. Since if there were any discrepancies between the conception, the form or the technique of his art, Moore, to whom as a direct carver the sculpture of the primitives inevitably appealed, could never have succeeded in the creation of a mode, which, though it is based on the formal principles of an archaic art, is yet the expression of a spirit and an attitude that is vital in his own time.

By a curious coincidence Henry Moore and Barbara Hepworth, the two outstanding sculptors in England today, were both born in Yorkshire and were both trained first of all at the School of Art in Leeds, and afterwards at the Royal College of Art in London. But while, in the earlier stages of their development, they had much in common, there is nothing in Hepworth's later work to indicate that she and Moore derived their original inspiration from similar sources.

Though not less concerned than Moore with the problem as to how to express in terms of sculpture that fundamental relationship which exists between man and woman and the landscape by which they are surrounded, Hepworth has never felt the need, since she reached the more mature period of her development as a sculptor, to express this relationship in other than abstract or semi-abstract terms. But because her forms are organized without reference to those that are specifically organic, they necessarily involve a more deliberate and precise consideration of purely formal problems. In her study of these problems, and especially of that concerning the inter-relationships of different forms,

[1] Extract from an essay which I contributed to *Werk*. April 1947.

she made a number of experiments between 1934 and 1937, sometimes using two and sometimes three shapes of varying size and complexity arranged on a base; and sometimes as in her *Conoid, Sphere and Hollow* making the base itself, by the emphasis of the hollow, an integral part of the carving. In speaking of this phase of her work, William Gibson has said in his monograph *Barbara Hepworth*[1] that there is also a variation of this style in which 'the relationships are not confined to the curves and proportions of the objects themselves, but include relationships between the latter and an imaginary object which they imply. The imaginary object is a simpler mass of which the carvings are variations by subtraction or addition.' This view he goes on to amplify by reference to *Pierced Hemisphere*, a fine carving in white marble which she executed towards the end of this period. 'The object actually presented', he says, 'implies the half sphere from which it varies by the piercing of a hole, the cutting away of the step and the rounding of part of the edge; and it is only when its proportions are imagined in relationship to the implied hemisphere that they acquire their full meaning.'

With the development of the stringed figure at the beginning of the present decade, she was able to express these relationships in a new form, but except in the finest examples such as *Pelagos* and *The Wave*, in which she has used this device with consummate effect, the heightened tension that was thereby gained was apt at times to be at the expense of the more enduring qualities of sculptural form.

Another problem with which she has been much pre-occupied is that of the re-introduction of colour into sculpture. 'I have been very influenced by the natural colour and luminosity of stones,' she once wrote, while in speaking of her practice of applying the colour to the concave rather than to the convex surfaces of her forms, she went on to say, 'When I pierced the material right through a great change seemed to take place in the concavities from which direct light was excluded. From this experience my use of colour developed.'[2] Though having a preference for the paler shades of pink, blue, yellow and grey, she has also employed blues of a deeper tone, but more often still she has shown a predilection for white. This she has used sometimes in conjunction with coloured strings and sometimes without, but rarely with greater effect than in *Elegy*, a carving which, just perhaps by reason of its quietness, has had a wide appeal. Even the curves, as someone once remarked, have a quality of tenderness about them, a quality which is intuitively felt by the beholder with the sensibility to feel these things, whether he is familiar with them and aware of their implications or not. For despite its abstraction and the apparent austerity of its form, Barbara Hepworth's art is born of a passion that is as profound as it is vital. Though seeming perhaps at first to be remote from the world of nature, it is yet the offspring of an intimate association with it—an association that has been deepened and intensified since she returned to life in the country—for it is against the sea and the landscape of Cornwall, a county that has much in common with her native Yorkshire, that the carvings of recent years must be imagined. And that her art is not divorced from reality is borne out by her own saying, 'One can experience the colour changes in nature in a cave, a forest or a pool and sense similar change in the emotional effect of all forms when the quantity and quality of light playing upon it changes.'[3] In other words, her aim has been neither to reproduce nor to represent nature, but *to recreate her experience of nature* in formal terms, which, though they may not be in accord with the perceptions of the common man, are nevertheless in harmony with the abstract tendencies of the age.

Even if sculpture were a more popular and a less difficult art than it is, it would be rare to find in any country more than one or two sculptors of genius within a generation and it is therefore a cause

[1] *Barbara Hepworth* by William Gibson. Faber & Faber. London, 1945.

[2] *The Studio*, London, 1946: 'Approach to Sculpture' by Barbara Hepworth.

[3] *Op. cit.*

of national pride that already in this century England should have produced two sculptors of the quality of Henry Moore and Barbara Hepworth. For although, as in most countries, there is a moderately sound academic tradition which the majority of sculptors are content to follow, it is not among those who have no original contribution to make to the sum total of sculptural achievement that the formative influences for the future can be sought. Yet as between the traditional type of sculpture, associated with the names of Sir William Reid Dick and Charles Wheeler, and that of the modern school, represented by Henry Moore and Barbara Hepworth, there is also a certain amount of work that is neither wholly figurative nor wholly non-figurative, but is midway between the two and is such that it would, unquestionably, be repudiated by the exponents of both schools. Among the artists who have produced work in this transitional style Leon Underwood, Barbara Austin-Taylor and Maurice Lambert may be included, while of the younger men who are looking more certainly towards the ideals of the modern school there are F. E. McWilliam and Robert Adams, of whom McWilliam has been influenced to some extent by Moore, though his work is rapidly becoming unrecognizable by Moore's standards, while Adams, who has been influenced by both Moore and Hepworth, possesses a sense of scale and a feeling for material which augurs well for his development in the future.

As far as her approach to sculpture is concerned, Belgium has shown herself to be more conservative than almost any other country in Europe. With two notable exceptions, those of her sculptors who have not remained faithful to the neo-classical ideals which, since they were established under the influence of Canova in the nineteenth century, have come to be regarded as traditional, have been content to continue rather than to advance those of the more modern modes which they have adopted. So that, although Belgium has produced a number of sculptors in recent times as her public monuments bear witness, she has made few original contributions to the art of the present century.

There are, however, these two notable exceptions, for as Marguerite Devigne has said, 'If the supreme expression of the age of naturalism may be found in the work of Meunier, that of our own epoch, which is pre-eminently one of sincerity, may be found in the work of George Minne.'[1]

Sooner or later, some reaction against the artificialities of a way of life that belongs to the past was bound to come, and to manifest itself in the art no less than in the lives of the people; but like Van Gogh, it was not until he visited the Belgian coalfields towards the end of his life that Constantin Meunier, who was to become the great exponent of social realism in sculpture, discovered his vocation. Before 1885, Meunier had worked only as a painter, but from that time onwards, until his death in 1905, sculpture became his sole interest and pre-occupation. Himself a child of poverty and suffering, he felt a natural sympathy for the working man in his toils and it was accordingly to the portrayal of miners, puddlers, glassblowers and other familiar and unfamiliar figures among the industrial classes that he was irresistibly attracted. But if his choice of subject was new to sculpture, the naturalism of his manner was even more of an innovation, providing, as it did, a startling contrast to the histrionics with which sculpture had previously been associated. Meunier's art was therefore a revolutionary art in more senses than one, yet even if it had been less completely in accord with the growing socialism of the age, its formative influence would still have been considerable, since it constituted a reaction against the conventions of the past that was at least as necessary as it was violent. But while his art belongs rather to the nineteenth than to the twentieth century, so that a fuller discussion of its

[1] *La Sculpture Belge*, 1830-1930, by Marguerite Devigne. Brussels, 1930.

22

merits would be out of place here, something of the bold, uncompromising character of his style is reflected in the *Self Portrait* of Rik Wouters, who from his obvious command of his medium might have achieved much had he not died at the early age of thirty-four in 1916.

The art of George Minne, on the other hand, was born of an entirely different spirit and is altogether more personal in feeling. Though it possesses nothing of Meunier's naturalism, Minne's art is nevertheless as direct an expression of his artistic creed as any expression of an attitude that is essentially spiritual could be. So that if in some instances he may appear to be straining after an effect that is barely to be realized in concrete terms, this is due not to any lack of sincerity on the sculptor's part, but rather to the intensity of the emotion which he sought to express. For Minne's mysticism, which was tinged perhaps with something of the same elusive quality as that which belongs to the symbolist writings of his friend Maeterlinck, was not of a kind that is easily expressible in sculptural form. Yet strange and unaccountable though his melancholy may be, it is simply and movingly conveyed in the beautiful image of his *Relic Bearer* which is as satisfactory on formal grounds as it is convincing from a religious standpoint.

Minne was not, however, ostensibly a religious artist, though such figures as his *Nun* and some of his numerous portrayals of the mother and child might well be thought to be religious in inspiration.

Except for a year when he studied at the Academie des Beaux Arts in Brussels under the well-known sculptor Van der Stappen, Minne worked mainly on his own. As a young man, he had visited Paris in the hope of being able to work in Rodin's studio, but on the advice of the great Frenchman he returned to Belgium, where except for a visit to England, where he took refuge during the 1914-18 War, he spent the rest of his life. Yet although his studio at Laetham, near Ghent, where he settled in 1899, became the centre of an important artistic group, Minne was by temperament a solitary, as Rodin probably recognized when he said, 'Such is the monumentality of your work that there is nothing I can teach you, neither I nor anyone else. Work on your own. You will succeed.'[1] If, therefore, Minne is great as a sculptor, it is not so much because of the influence he has had on the development of the sculpture of his period, as because of the intensely individual quality of his own achievement.

To turn from so highly personal an art as Minne's to the derivative art of Egide Rombeaux, accomplished though it is, is to discover the fundamental difference between the great and the good. Since, although Rodin's style, from which Rombeaux's is derived, is a style which lends itself to imitation where Minne's does not, the spirit by which it was inspired is not communicable in the sense that it can be identified in the work of another who has little if anything of his own to contribute. In the same way, it is difficult to see in what the value of a figure like Charles Leplae's *Luco* finally consists, seeing that it might have been produced by almost any sculptor of any period who possessed the necessary technical ability. In other words, to assimilate the lessons of a Rodin or of a Despiau is not in itself enough to justify the work of a sculptor, whose claims to recognition rest on quite other grounds than these. But Belgian tendencies in sculpture being what they are, it is easy to see why it is the sound but relatively unspectacular work of Maillol and Despiau as opposed to that of Rodin or of the more extreme moderns that has made the deepest impression upon the artists of the present generation.

The history of twentieth century sculpture in Czechoslovakia has been dominated by the genius of J. V. Myslbec. Nearly every artist of repute has either been trained in his studio or has come under

[1] *George Minne* by Leo van Puyvelde. Brussels, 1930.

his influence in one way or another, 'being drawn, again and again, through the magnetism of his creative personality, to the master's works, no matter how far they may venture from his realistic monumentality'.

From the outset and even in those of his early works in which he still remained under the prevailing influence of the nineteenth century, Myslbec showed himself to be no ordinary sculptor, whose promise was revealed in both the assurance of his manner and the fluency of his style. Nor in later life did this early promise remain unfulfilled, for whether it be in the execution of religious sculpture, of portraiture or of public monuments to which the dramatic qualities of his style with its freedom of gesture are eminently suited, the same exuberance and the same forcefulness remain evident; though it is in such a work as his statue of *Cardinal Swarzenberg* that his unique sense of character is most notably exhibited.

But while he possessed something of the same kind of creative energy as Rodin, Myslbec did not introduce any fundamental stylistic or technical changes, as the French master had done, but based his teaching on the traditional canons of his art, as these were generally understood. Indeed, being opposed to the practice of Impressionism in sculpture, his studio inevitably became the centre of the reaction against it. Yet although Rodin ultimately failed to convert Czech sculptors to a belief in his method he nevertheless attracted a number to his studio and exerted an unmistakable influence upon the development of others. This may be seen not only in the work of a convinced Impressionist like Jozef Kostka, but also in certain examples of the work of such men as Jan Lauda, who was a pupil of Stursa's and works in various styles, and Karel Pokorný, a pupil of Myslbec himself, who in his *Head of Christ* in the Prague National Gallery clearly proclaims his debt to Rodin, for it would be difficult to find a bronze that more strikingly exemplifies 'the art of the hump and the hollow'.

But in sculpture as in painting the influence of the Ecole de Paris upon the evolution of modern art in Czechoslovakia has been considerable, though even in the case of those sculptors like Otto Gutfreund and Vincenc Makovský, for instance, who have passed through all the experimental phases of cubism, surrealism and constructivism, a final return to traditional means and methods has shown where their true convictions lay. Nor, judged purely on their merits as sculpture, would it be difficult to say where the preference lies as between Gutfreund's *Don Quixote*, which is executed on lines similar to those on which Picasso's *Bronze Head* of 1909 is built up, though without that vigour which renders Picasso's use of the cubist manner convincing, and Makovský's unpretentious but sensitive *Portrait of the Artist Petr*, a work in complete contrast with the bolder and more famous portrait of *T. G. Masaryk*, but one with which, however, it may fittingly be compared.

Of all Myslbec's pupils, Jan Stursa was the most versatile and the most brilliant. In his youth he had been trained as a stonemason, but unlike Gill he was not exclusively or even primarily a carver, though one has only to consider his *Burial in the Carpathians*, a carving in pear wood of a group of soldiers with their dead comrade in the midst, which he executed after the last War, to perceive the completeness of his recognition of the need for economy and coherence in a design of this kind. It shows, too, a complete change of feeling and a deeper artistic purpose than that which had been evident in the work which he executed before the War. Even before that, however, his development had been marked by sudden changes, as when he turned from the rendering of youth and of youthful types and qualities to the portrayal of man or, more correctly, of woman (after the fashion of sculptors) in the fullness of her maturity albeit conceived only as a creature of animal lusts, a being without a soul, to whom the distinctions of personality are denied; it was, in any case, in types rather than in individuals (apart from his portraiture) that Stursa was mainly interested. That is to say, his approach to sculpture was on the whole objective, for even in his *Wounded Warrior*, which marks the beginning of his post-war period and is evidently inspired by a different spirit from that by which he was animated before, one is less moved by the subject than interested in the technical problem of balance which it involves, this being one with which Stursa appears to have been particuary concerned. Yet that he is capable of a deeper power of expression is shown, for example, in the *Bust of the Artist's Mother*, a work of great tenderness and restraint, in which there is a subtle adjustment between the minuteness of the surface treatment and the breadth of the scale on which the work is conceived.

In addition to his portrait-busts and his nudes, which are executed in both stone and bronze, Stursa is also famous for his commemorative sculpture and public monuments. Yet even so one cannot feel, in view of his various changes of style and the range of his accomplishment, that he had reached the limit of his capacity at the age of forty-five, when in 1925 after a long and painful illness he ended by taking his own life.

Sculpture in Finland is pre-eminently the art of granite carving and it is to this difficult task that the majority of Finnish sculptors have from time to time turned their attention. As might be expected, however, in a land of forests like Finland, wood carving, which is derived from a folk art, has also been extensively practised.

During the political and artistic renaissance which took place at the beginning of the nineteenth century, when Finland ceased to be a Swedish dependency after five hundred years, a period in which artistic activity seems to have been increased rather than diminished by the subsequent attempts of Russia to dominate the country, sculpture was to the fore in the person of Erik Cainberg, a pupil of the Swedish sculptor, Sergel, though it was under the leadership of another Swede, Carl Sjöstrand, who had settled in Finland, that modern Finnish sculpture was developed. Up to this time, it had been towards Rome and towards Copenhagen, the city of Thorwaldsen, that the few sculptors that Finland produced had looked for their inspiration. But from 1876 onwards, according to Onni Okkonen,[1] when Walter Runeberg, a son of the national poet and the first modern Finnish sculptor of importance, turned from Rome to Paris where he came in contact with the growing realism of the French school for the first time, a gradual change in the sculptural style of Finland may be detected, where as in other countries in Europe a taste for realism took the place of the post-classical ideals that had formerly prevailed. But while the value of realism as an end in itself may easily be over-estimated, the importance of the freedom for the exercise of other faculties to which it led could hardly be exaggerated, considering the variety of sculptural attainments to which it ultimately gave rise.

The most commanding name in Finnish sculpture today is that of Wäinö Aaltonen, who is at once both carver and modeller, *busteur* and idealist, and whose range of work in a variety of mediums makes him one of the outstanding figures in the contemporary field.

As a sculptor, he was, however, largely self-taught, since it was only after he had completed his studies as a painter at the Ecole des Beaux Arts, Turku, that his interest in sculpture developed. Yet notwithstanding the distinctiveness of his style, certain influences are from time to time detectable in his work, whether of Rodin or Rosso or some other master by whose work he may temporarily have been attracted. In his incisive portrait of *Sibelius*, for instance, he would appear to owe something to Rodin in his method of presentation, though there is presumably this difference in the work, that

[1] *L'Art Finlandais* by Onni Okkonen. Helsinki, 1938.

25

whereas Rodin's carvings were executed from the clay model by assistants working in his studio, Aaltonen's will presumably have been carved direct, though according to Kineton Parkes[1] he is in the habit of using the pointer if and when the occasion requires it.

Although he has produced a number of carvings in wood and in marble, mostly of female heads and figures, among which his *Wader* is perhaps outstanding, Aaltonen's main interest, as with so many Finnish sculptors, has been in the carving of granite, a medium which he has used with notable success in his kneeling *Warrior*, the giant figure at Savonlinna which he carved as a Memorial to those who fell in the War of Independence, when Finland won her freedom from Russia in 1918. But if as a carver Aaltonen is impressive, he is no less so as a modeller, as his figure of *Paavo Nurmi* bears witness, for there are few renderings of speed which for sheer skill in the co-ordination of the movement are equal to this.

Other Finnish sculptors who may be mentioned include the wood carvers, Emil Halonen and Hannes Autere, both of whom have specialized in work in relief; Johannes Haapsalo, who in his carvings in marble and granite has produced work in the typical European tradition, his nudes being pleasing rather than original; and Yrjö Liipola who is primarily a modeller, whose figures, including the Rodinesque *Awakening Strength* have a naturalness that is satisfactory rather than new.

But if no account of Finnish art, however brief, would be complete without mention of the animalier J. Mäntynen, whose carvings of the lynx and the bear may be justly described as superb, the same might be said in regard to many of the animaliers in other countries, since there are few that have not produced artists of merit in this field.

Auguste Rodin was born in 1840. In 1876 his *Man with a Broken Nose* (which had been refused in 1864) was exhibited at the Salon and a new era in sculpture had begun. For although, as Epstein has remarked, 'every schoolboy now seems able to pick holes in him', it was Rodin 'who compelled sculpture into paths which it is still following or which have developed from his fecund example'.

Although he studied first under the French animalier Barye and afterwards under the Belgian sculptor Van Rasbourg, it was from neither the one nor the other that Rodin received the final impulse to his genius, but rather, according to Louis Vauxcelles, from Medardo Rosso, whose work he may perhaps have seen during his first visit to Italy in 1875. But whether this is so or not, for the two men undoubtedly had something in common, it is certainly from the Impressionism of Manet in painting and of Rodin and Rosso in sculpture that the modern movement in art takes its rise.

Unlike Stursa or even Aaltonen, Rodin shows a consistency in his development that marks him out as the greatest individualist of his period. At the same time, being a modeller by instinct, while his themes were not on the whole of a kind that lent themselves to a glyptic interpretation, his attention and interest remained undivided, since, as has already been said, his works in stone were carried out in the studio at the hands of others. Obsessed with the conviction that 'it is simply the power of character that makes for beauty in art', he put the whole passionate energy of which he was capable into the expression of ideas, which some, after the fashion of today, would stigmatize as 'literary' but which others, without begging the question, would justify as 'poetic'. For, whether we translate a feeling or a conviction into words and say, 'Who knoweth not in all these things that the hand of the Lord hath wrought this? In whose hand is the soul of every living thing, and the breath of all

[1] *The Art of Carved Sculpture* by Kineton Parkes. Chapman & Hall. London, 1931.

mankind', or whether we translate this, or an equivalent creative conception, into visible form as Rodin has done in his *Hand of God*, it makes no matter. What *does* matter and what *is* important is that the work should be consonant with the formal principles of the art which it exemplifies, and that it should be *expressive*, which is above all the criterion that Rodin himself would have proposed.

Proceeding on this assumption and accepting Rodin's criterion as a basis, it may accordingly be said that, considered as a whole, there are few achievements in sculpture more expressive than his; yet while in his finest work form and content, passion and coherence are reconciled, in the realization of some of the less innately sculptural conceptions, that is to say, in conceptions like *The Gates of Hell* and even perhaps the *Burghers of Calais*, which are not inherently unified, there is a tendency either for the passion to outrun the form or else for the parts to be emphasized at the expense of the whole. The comparative failure of the *Prodigal Son*, for instance, as against the *Hand of God*, arises from the fact that the first is not fully expressive of the idea which is superimposed, the title presumably being given on the completion of the work, while the second represents a complete identification of form and content and is a work of outstanding originality and power.

To claim for Aristide Maillol a higher place than Rodin in the history of sculpture, simply on the ground that his work is more nearly in line with the tradition of pure sculpture, would be, in one sense, to mistake the means for the end. It is true that from a technical standpoint his art may be more perfect, yet even this hardly constitutes a legitimate basis of comparison, seeing that Rodin's technique in no way amounts to a failure to approximate to a preconceived norm, but is a technique that was deliberately used as being the only one adapted to the expression of his genius. But even if the superiority of Maillol's method as a modeller be allowed, the aridity of his imagination in comparison with the richness of Rodin's would in itself be sufficient to indicate that his powers as an artist, in the larger meaning of the term, belong to a different order. Where Rodin was preoccupied with the dynamic, Maillol, on his own admission, was originally concerned merely with the wish 'to carve a pretty shape'—a statement which shows more clearly than any comment the fundamental difference between the creative attitude of the two men.

But it was, after all, almost as if by chance that Maillol came to be a sculptor at all since, on the completion of his studies at the Ecole des Beaux Arts in Paris, he returned to the Midi with the intention of devoting himself to the production of tapestry, and it was only as the result of a temporary loss of his eyesight that he turned to sculpture as an alternative.

As his biographer, Marguerite Bouvier,[1] has said, however, he found himself at the outset as a sculptor in the creation of *la femme Maillol*, which he first realized in miniature, though later he turned to the modelling of life-size and occasionally of over life-sized figures, as in the great *Torso* in the Tate Gallery. But whether they be super-human as in the *Torso* or miniature as in Mr E. C. Gregory's *Woman Dressing her Hair*, which shows Maillol at his best, the modelling is superb in its classic simplicity and in the strength of its tactile appeal alike. But that Maillol's interest was centred exclusively in the body as opposed to the soul, is borne out by his entire concentration upon the rendering of voluptuous rounded forms (not, however, for the sake of their voluptuousness, but for the sake of their roundedness, volume not sex being his prepossession), as witness his request to Dina Vierny, who served as his model for the last seven years of his life—'I hear you have the figure of *la femme Maillol*; will you come and pose for me?'

But what makes Maillol's work monotonous, apart from the fact that he remained content to model the same figure for nearly forty-two years, with only an occasional variation, is the sameness of his

[1] *Aristide Maillol* by Marguerite Bouvier. Lausanne, 1945.

heads, together with the fact that he entirely 'neglected the inner life of his creatures'. So that for all the suavity of their outward form, his *Three Nymphs*, which he executed towards the end of his career, remain passionless in the studiedness of their remote neo-classical perfection, though it is perhaps just because of the impersonal perfection by which his work is characterized that his method has been found worthy of emulation in nearly every country in Europe.

A sculptor who has had a comparable influence in his own field and who in his concentration upon the inner life of his subjects provides a perfect counterpart to Maillol is Charles Despiau, the *busteur par excellence* of his period in France. A sculptor of limited range, he achieved within those limits a classical purity of style that proclaims the essential artist, though owing to the inequality of his performance there is a considerable difference of opinion as to its final importance. Yet while much of what he produced is accomplished rather than inspired, there seems little doubt that at his best he is a sculptor of unusual sensibility, whose feeling for form is expressed in the fineness of the plastic quality of his heads, as may be seen, for instance, in his *Petite Fille des Landes*, an early work of great simplicity and charm, and in *Paulette*, a work of later date, which show, the one no less than the other, how perfectly the sympathy and restraint of his manner was suited to the portrayal of women.

Henri Gaudier-Brzeska, who spent the greater part of his short life in England, was an enthusiastic exponent of the *taille directe* method, which had been advocated and developed in France towards the end of the last century by Josef Bernard. As may be seen from the small carving here reproduced, which shows the influence of Negro sculpture on his work, his preoccupation with masses and with 'the defining of these masses by planes', a preoccupation which led him towards an increasingly abstract interpretation of his subject, is clearly evident. Unfortunately, his early promise was never fulfilled, but the little that he had accomplished when in 1915 he was killed in France at the age of twenty-four is enough to show how great a loss the art of sculpture sustained through his premature death.

With this carving by Gaudier-Brzeska Henri Laurens's terra-cotta, *Jockey*, may usefully be compared, as being a development of the tendencies inherent in the negro mode, by which Laurens, like other Cubists, was decisively influenced. But as George L. K. Morris has pointed out, 'unlike most sculptors associated with the movement, Laurens followed the paintings closely in his wooden reliefs', and for that matter also in his free-standing figures, as may be seen from the work illustrated. In some of his more recent work, on the other hand, he has been occupied with a semi-naturalistic and sometimes with a naturalistic treatment of the human figure, though naturalistic, be it understood, in the sense in which the term might be used with reference to the figures in some of Picasso's paintings of about 1922 and not in the sense in which it would have been understood in the nineteenth century.

To Jean Arp, one of the most advanced members of the modern movement in Europe, the question of truth to nature would not present itself as a relevant artistic consideration at all, since it is with problems of an entirely different order that he is concerned.

As one of the founders of the pre-surrealist movement known as Dada, Arp was in the forefront of the moderns before the end of the last War, but his natural taste has been more nearly satisfied by the exercises in abstract and semi-abstract form to which he later turned his attention. Even as recently as 1936, however, he was still sufficiently interested in the surrealist 'object' to contrive his *Mutilé et Apatride*, which provides a sharp contrast to some of his other work of the same period—the carved and painted reliefs, a form of sculpture in which the nicety of his feeling for subtly related shapes is manifest—and in the direct carvings in the round, which are no less characteristic.

In these, which are commonly entitled *Concrétion Humaine*, he makes no attempt to simplify the human form on Brancusi's lines of progressive refinement, but while basing his motifs on the 'feel' of the body, proceeds to evolve shapes and forms that retain their likeness to nature only in the fleshly character of their volume and in the 'softness' of their tactile appeal which tends, however, to be too great to be sculpturally satisfactory. His exquisite *Sculpture Méditerranéenne* of 1941 is, on the other hand, a work of pure sculpture, being as taut in tension, as it is subtle in balance and perfect in form, so that like the *Sculpture Conjugale*, which he executed in association with his wife, the late Sophie Tauber-Arp, an artist of great sensibility and taste, it is a carving that commands instant recognition as a work of art.

In spite of the experimental nature of her genius and the natural abstruseness of her thought, Germany has contributed less to the evolution of abstract art than one would have expected, especially as it was at Weimar that the Bauhaus was originally founded by Walter Gropius immediately after the last war. But whether because of the repression of the modern movement under the totalitarian tyranny, because the influence of tradition was too strong, or because abstraction in art is finally distasteful to the Teutonic imagination, it is certain that the representative sculptors of modern Germany are neither Richard Haizmann, whose abstraction has something in common with Brancusi's, nor Rudolph Belling, whose constructivism, though it owes little if anything to the Russian school, has certain affinities with it, nor Karl Schmidt-Rottluff, whose plastic modes are inspired largely by his feeling for material, but rather Georg Kolbe, Wilhelm Lehmbruck and Ernst Barlach, all of whom have developed along traditional lines.

In view of the extreme differences of style which they represent, opinions must necessarily differ as to which sculptor is to be preferred, but it will generally be agreed that Georg Kolbe was the least original. Yet, while there is nothing particularly individual in his treatment of the nude (this being the study in which he was exclusively interested as a sculptor) and while the modelling may at times be coarse and even clumsy, the total effect is such that one is less conscious of minor defects than of the sense of strength and liberation that the work conveys. This is due partly to the feeling of weight which Kolbe almost invariably captures, a feeling that is of the utmost importance in sculpture but is only rarely achieved, and partly to the straightforward and uninhibited spirit of his approach. This may be seen, for example, in the undifferentiated manner of his handling of the two figures that are reproduced, of which the first is *The Genius of Beethoven*, a detail of an uncompleted project, and the second a detail of his *Young Man Stepping Forward*. That is to say, his work betrays no adolescent interest or curiosity, but is wholly asexual, the body, whether male or female, being but the form through which a certain quality of inward grace is expressed.

Though interested primarily in the pose as against the actual movement of a figure, Kolbe is famous above all for his *Dancer*, which is one of the most captivating examples of rhythmic movement that modern sculpture has produced, and is unusual as far as the rest of Kolbe's own achievement is concerned, the majority of his figures, which include commemorative figures of one kind or another, being poised as if *about* to move forward, but not actually doing so, which of all positions in sculpture is one of the more effective.

In comparison with Kolbe's art, that of Wilhelm Lehmbruck is altogether softer and more seductive. But whereas Kolbe had shown little variation of style throughout his long life as a sculptor Lehmbruck, who took his own life at the age of thirty-eight in 1919, and can scarcely have produced more than a fragment of the work of which he may ultimately have been capable, had passed through a variety of phases before attaining a highly individual style of his own. Though he came under the influence of Maillol during his visit to Paris in 1910, as the work of that period indicates, he had by nature closer affinities with the mysticism of the gothic spirit and it is not therefore surprising to find that it was in the art of George Minne that he discovered his final inspiration. But whatever he assimilated from the art of the great Belgian he interpreted in his own way, his forms being on the whole more attenuated and less impassioned than Minne's, and his manner as distinctive.

Although both are apt to give an unwonted air of sentimentality to the work, the two features that are typical of Lehmbruck's style are the elongated form and the inclined head, both of which are seen in the accompanying *Bust* of a woman, which has, however, a certain decisiveness and formal grace about it that is wholly pleasing. This inclination of the head occurs again in his *Kneeling Woman*, the over life-size figure that is generally regarded as his masterpiece, a figure that in spite of the somewhat precious form of its pose and its lack of contemporary feeling has excited universal admiration. Yet perhaps after all it is not an interpretation of the modern spirit that is sought in this connection, since it is in all probability just because of its flavour of medievalism and its remoteness from the world of today that Lehmbruck's work has proved so attractive to his compatriots. Similarly, there is nothing in the quiet unmodernness of the figures of Gerhardt Marcks, a sculptor who is little known outside Germany, but who has a considerable reputation in his own country, to indicate that he was once a director of the ceramic department of the Bauhaus, from which it may be assumed that he would not at one time have considered a work such as his *Girl with an Apple* as definitive.

But of all German sculptors of the twentieth century Ernst Barlach, who died in 1939, is probably the most popular, for as Peter Thoene has said, 'his sculpture is German through and through, uniting the oldest source of the Nordic interpretation of life with the latter-day will of Expressionism'.[1] In other words, Barlach was an artist who was at once a social realist and a visionary, whose consciousness of man's sufferings and whose awareness of the unseen powers by which he is surrounded is expressed with equal forcefulness in his wood-carvings and in the poetic dramas with which his name is also associated.

It was, however, in Russia and in the vastness of the Russian landscape that he came to realize man's loneliness in the midst of nature, just as it was in the attitude of the Russian peasant that he recognized a fatalism comparable with his own, for it was his sense of human isolation and of human destiny that he contrived to embody in his art, in a form that may justly be described as unique. Thus, by making the base an integral part of the composition, he succeeded in relating his figures to their setting and thereby of emphasizing their remoteness in a way that is rare in sculpture, while by posing them in such a manner that the play of the elements or the presence of some impending fate is automatically suggested, he was able to heighten the intensity of whatever sentiment he sought to convey. Again, by using the same style of chip carving in the treatment of the figures, their garments and their setting, he managed to achieve a unity that is as distinctive as it is apt to be monotonous.

This may be seen in two contrasted works, *The Avenger* and *Panic-stricken* ('*Panischer Schrecken*'), which are equally characteristic, though it is interesting to note that while the mood changes from active to passive, there is little appreciable change of method, which in these, as in many similar examples, is directly expressive of his creed. For despite the mixture of naïveté and sophistication in his nature, Barlach was patently sincere, as the inherent simplicity of his work bears witness; moreover, as he himself has said, 'Reluctantly enough, I began to leave out everything that could not help to strengthen the effect I had clearly conceived', a statement in which the attitude of the true artist is

[1] *Modern German Art* by Peter Thoene, translated by Charles Fullman. Penguin Books Ltd. London, 1938.

in the Uffizzi is notable; Libero Andreotti, Attilio Silva and Evaristo Bonciuelli, who belong to the realist school; and Arturo Martini, a pupil of Hildebrand's, whose work is everything that sculpture should not be, notwithstanding the fact that he, together with Ernesto di Fiori, has been described as a liberator of Italian sculpture.

Seeing, then, that so much Italian work continues to conform to conventional patterns of one kind or another, it is a relief to turn to the work of an original artist like Umberto Boccioni, a member of the Futurist movement, which understandably enough in view of the stultification into which a continual repetition of outworn formulae is apt to lead, professed 'a horror of everything old and known'. But here again, painting was the art that lent itself more readily to the solution of the new problems of the rendering of movement and of 'the particular rhythm of each object, its inclination . . . and interior force', though Boccioni undoubtedly succeeded in capturing this 'dynamic sensation' in his remarkable *Striding Figure* of 1913. So that if after his death in 1916 Futurism failed to produce any further work on these lines, this must be attributed at least as much to the fact that sculptors of Boccioni's genius are not born in every generation, as to the claim that sculpture is inherently unsuited to experiments of this kind. But that a less conventional approach to sculptural problems, albeit of a different type, is being made is seen in the semi-abstract *Torso* of 1945 by a young Venetian sculptor, Alberto Viani, who is interested in the study of plastic form on severely sculptural lines, in the pursuit of which he has evolved a form reminiscent of the more accomplished work of Jean Arp, which in all probability, however, he has never seen.

To all intents and purposes, the sculpture of Jugoslavia is fully represented by the art of Ivan Meštrović and Toma Rosandić, of whom Meštrović is the more widely known. Indeed, Meštrović, who is one of the few artists whom fortune seems to have favoured from the outset, enjoys an international reputation that is second only to that of Rodin.

Like a great many sculptors, Meštrović, who was born in Dalmatia in 1883, came of peasant stock, his father, from whom he learnt the rudiments of his craft, being connected with the building trade. Later on at the age of fifteen he was apprenticed to a master mason in Spalato, or Split, to use the modern name, where in the ruins of Diocletian's palace he was afterwards to see his colossal figure of *Bishop Gregory of Nin* set up. For like all the art of communities which have suffered under foreign domination, the art of Serbia, as it then was, was an intensely national art, and Meštrović, whose imagination as a boy had been stirred by the legends of the heroes of Kossova, which were still sung by the blind guslar singers until the time of the last war, naturally tended to conceive his figures on an heroic scale. This is seen for instance in his torso *Strahanić Ban*, an imposing example of his art, which was presented to the Victoria and Albert Museum by the Serbian Government at Meštrović's own wish.

Unlike most modern sculptors Meštrović has had the opportunity not only of exercising his art in relation to architecture, but also of designing the buildings for which much of his work was conceived, as in the case of the Temple at Kossova, which commemorates the heroes who fell in the battle of that name in 1389, and in the Mortuary Chapel of the Racic family at Cavtat, which he completed in 1922.

In the latter, his accomplishment as a religious artist is seen to the full. But if, as is habitually claimed, his work is strongly Byzantine in character, it is even more Meštrovićian, if one might so say, since whether he is treating a religious or a secular subject his manner remains the same, while the work is not infused with a spirit that is perceptibly different. Admittedly, the work is invariably stylized and aloof, to which extent it might be conceived as an hieratic art, but for all its coldness, it retains a distinctly personal flavour, while his types are always recognizably his own. Thus the *Lute Player*, which is one of his finest and most effective carvings, bears a strong resemblance to certain of his Madonnas, in addition to which his treatment of the hands, especially in the later work, is nearly always the same. So that although he has executed both portrait busts and groups of the mother and child, his genius being what it is, he would seem to be suited to the creation of work of a formal, rather than of an intimate character.

A notable example of his work in relief is given in the Canadian War Memorial, in which this gift for formalized design is exercised to perfection, whereas his *Descent from the Cross*, a relief in wood which is now in the Tate Gallery, reveals at once his inability to organize a scene that cannot be rigidly formalized and a lack of that all-embracing humanity, which an artist of Meštrović's stature might be expected to possess.

Toma Rosandić, who is more of a craftsman and less of *un grand maître* than Meštrović, is an artist of much greater warmth and intimacy, who has achieved a number of carvings, especially in wood, in which the simplicity of his approach is evident. Although he owes something perhaps to Meštrović, with whom he worked in Vienna, his work, though stylized up to a point, is much less severely disciplined perhaps because as a direct carver he has less need to define his aims explicitly from the outset. For although Meštrović is himself both a carver and a modeller, it is not to be expected, in view of the amount of work he has produced, that he should have executed everything himself without the assistance of the formatore. Unfortunately, however, Rosandić's work is little known in England, though he held an exhibition of his work in London in 1919.

The career of Gustav Vigeland is one of the anomalies of the century. He was born at Mandal in Norway in 1869 and was apprenticed to a wood-carver in Oslo at the age of fourteen. Five years later he entered the studio of the Norwegian sculptor Brynjulf Bergslien, who considered the boy to be a genius and on the strength of his drawings even persuaded a group of professors to pay for his keep.

From the start, Vigeland's ideas appear to have been on a large scale and for many years he endured the uttermost extremes of poverty in the pursuit of his aims. But nothing daunted him; neither the physical privations which he suffered nor the adverse criticisms which his work aroused from the time of his first exhibition in 1894. It was, however, with the project for a fountain, which he undertook immediately after the completion of the Abel Monument of 1905, that Vigeland's life's work began. In speaking of this design, Kn. Aamot, the chairman of the Vigeland Committee, has written, 'That this design aroused attention is a mild expression. It called forth an enthusiasm and an opposition, a fanatical admiration and a scornful abuse which would seem almost impossible in our latitudes. Never has an artist caused such a blast as Vigeland with his first fountain.' It was estimated that the fountain would cost 300,000 kroner and would take ten years to produce, but this did not deter his supporters and in 1907 the first Vigeland Committee was formed for collecting the necessary funds. From then onwards, the project grew and 'in order to procure money for this large extension of plans, a new committee was formed in 1917'. And that no mean supply of funds was needed may be judged from the description which Aamot gives as follows: 'Vigeland proposed that . . . a large semi-circular granite stairway should lead up to the plateau where the fountain should be placed. Round the fountain an open square would spread, paved with stone in a labyrinth pattern. Round the whole structure a stone balustrade would be built, containing twenty-eight granite figures. From the fountain plateau, steps should lead down to a lower plateau forming a broad passage round the whole layout. From there and down to Karl Jogansgt, broad steps would lead and on pedestals on these stairs were to be placed forty large granite groups in ten radial rows.' As Vigeland had no means of procuring himself the necessary studio for such a work he finally 'decided to write to the State and offer all his work on condition that the State built a studio where he could work and where his work could find a place for posterity', as a result of which a contract embodying these proposals was drawn up in 1921. Thus the Vigeland studio was built at Grogner Park at the cost of two and a quarter million kroner, which was defrayed from the profits of Oslo Cinematographs. The work was not completed until over twenty years later, but at the time of his death early in 1943, Vigeland was still talking of all the work he proposed to do. What, however, is more amazing than the project itself, is that any municipality should have been got to pay for it; since it remains today, as at its inception, a matter of fierce dispute, which, again, is less amazing than that critical opinion should be divided. Yet, as the Director of the Committee has said, 'The efforts to destroy Vigeland's splendid work were unsuccessful, but . . . even as late as 1945 fanatical opponents of Vigeland found space in the Oslo Press for a proposal that the whole Vigeland plant should be razed!'[1]

In speaking of the Central Monument Evelyn Waugh, who had the opportunity of visiting the Park, describes it as being 'a vast monolith, explicitly and uncompromisingly phallic, on which converge bridges and avenues lined with a multitudinous sub-human zoo in bronze and granite, representing the cycles of life from embryo to skeleton. . . . It is a stupendous achievement and in all that mass of writhing muscle there is no hint anywhere of any intellectual process or spiritual aspiration.'

A stupendous achievement—or rather, a stupendous undertaking which can only be regarded as a disaster, as much for Vigeland as for Norway, and the only pity is that the municipality should have been persuaded to finance it, since it is not a scheme that could ever have been realized even by an artist of overwhelming genius, and the very fact that Vigeland supposed that it could have been possible shows his lack of an understanding of the very nature of sculpture, just as his so-called *Tree of Life*, on which some ten children 'cluster like grapes', to quote but one example, reveals his ignorance of its formal principles. Yet that he was a man of prodigious energy no one can doubt, while that he had at moments a sense of style and even a certain originality of conception is borne out by his memorial to *Henrik Wergeland*, the 'Byron of Norway', and it is thence the more regrettable that his abilities should have been so singularly misdirected.

Of the many younger sculptors of Norway, Emil Lie is considered by his countrymen to be one of the finest. But although he has studied and worked in France, in Italy and in England, he seems to have remained entirely uninfluenced by the various 'isms' with which he must have come in contact during his travels. This may be accounted for by the complete objectivity of his approach and by his preference for an entirely naturalistic treatment of his subject. So that if he has been influenced at all by foreign masters, it is by the work of Maillol that he would appear to have been most affected and, on external evidence, it is certainly to the art of the great Frenchman that he might have been expected to be attracted. In any case, he undoubtedly displays something of the same feeling for volume, particularly in his figure of a *Young Woman* in the National Gallery at Oslo, and in certain of his reclining figures. He is seen perhaps to rather less advantage in the *Seated Boy*, which is reproduced,

[1] *Vigeland* by Kr. Aamot and Niels F. Schach. Oslo.

though even here the straightforwardness of his approach and the strongness of his liking for firm, rounded limbs, a liking which proclaims his instinct as a modeller, is evident.

Of the art of all the moderns that of the Rumanian sculptor, Constantin Brancusi, is at once the purest and the most logical. He begins with nature and through a process of simplification that excludes everything that is not *absolutely* relevant to his purpose, transforms the object of his contemplation into a work of art. That is to say, he carries Cézanne's notion of the geometrical basis of all natural forms to its ultimate conclusion, which is one of the reasons why Brancusi might be described as a sculptor's sculptor, no matter how arid or mechanical the results may seem to be to the uninitiated. For as Epstein said in answer to the question as to whether a mechanic could have made Brancusi's polished brass *Bird*, when a trial was held in America to decide whether it was a mechanical implement or a work of art and as such exempt from duty—'A mechanic could have polished this, but he could not have conceived it.' Such an art does not, of course, make for recognition by the vulgar, who, in matters of art, might more accurately be said 'to like what they know' than 'to know what they like'. But for all that Brancusi is one of the most important artists of the present century, both because of the intrinsic qualities of the work itself and because of the influence it has had on the development of modern trends. As a craftsman, too, he is exceptionally skilled as is proved by the fact that his *Endless Column*, which is part of the scheme which he conceived for the lay-out at Targu Iju in Rumania in 1938, is balanced in a few inches and not, as Giedon-Welcker has pointed out, at the sacrifice of about a third of its length, as might have been supposed. For in Brancusi, as in Hepworth and Moore, the complete craftsman and the essential artist are identified in such a way that the integrity of the one implies the perfection of the other, a proof of which is given in the *Torso of a Young Girl* and in *The New-Born*, of which the latter in the austerity of its conception and in the beauty of its finish affords an ideal example of Brancusi's genius.

To the experimental movements in modern art the sculptors of Russia, Lithuania and Poland have made some interesting and, occasionally, some important contributions, but it is noteworthy that few of them have remained in their own countries, those who are among the better known, of whom Archipenko, Zadkine, Pevsner and Lipchitz may be mentioned, having migrated sooner or later to Germany, France or America.

In speaking of the development of sculpture in his book, *The New Vision*, Moholy-Nagy recognizes five stages, namely, the blocked-out, the hollowed-out, the bored-through, the equipoised and the kinetic, or mobile. The credit for the second, 'the first conscious use of concaves in sculpture—to replace saliences', he assigns to Alexander Archipenko, who was born in 1887 at Kiev, where he studied for four years at an art school before he took his way to Paris and other art centres in Western Europe.

From the first Archipenko appears to have been opposed to all orthodox methods of expression, inasmuch as he contends that he has 'thoughts and ideas which nature's forms cannot project', but as the accompanying *Standing Figure* in terra-cotta shows, he takes his departure from nature, on the basis of which he makes such adaptations and adjustments as he finds to be necessary for his purpose, though these are, on the face of it, less understandable than Brancusi's simplifications. But Archipenko does not invariably remain even as close to nature as this, nor does he always work in the more usual materials of his art, but like other cubists, the group with which he was at one time closely associated, has employed a number of different materials in combination. But like the majority of sculptors he is at his best in the handling of simpler forms and media, though his *Mourning Women* is a striking example of his adaptation of the counterpoint method of the cubist painters to the art of sculpture, or to what has been more accurately described as sculpto-painting.

Osip Zadkine, whose style is largely derived from the study of African negro prototypes, is another sculptor who, both as a modeller and as a carver, has made an extensive use of the concave, which he uses as the direct counterpart of the convex surface. But while this method allows of a greater interplay, in true cubist fashion, between one form and another, as for instance between Orpheus and his lyre, it does not increase but rather diminishes the three-dimensional effect of the work as a whole. Moreover, used as Zadkine uses it, the concave inevitably tends to a technical weakening of the form, which, from a purist standpoint, must be acknowledged to constitute a defect, no matter how expressive a means it may provide for what the sculptor has to say; for in his *Harlequin*, a typical example of his work, it is obvious that he is using something in the nature of a new form-language, which enables him to express what could not have been expressed by a conventional treatment of the subject. As to technical considerations, there are, of course, other standpoints from that of the purist and in this connection Wilenski has written as follows: 'The technique of bronze sculpture has remained more or less the same for close on a thousand years. Zadkine has made most interesting attempts to enlarge experience in this technical field concurrently with the enlargement of experience in the field of abstract form.'[1] Thus in the process of evolution from the plastic to the constructive, the stage which such an art as Zadkine's represents is intermediate, just as in painting cubism was a transitional phase between post-impressionism and pure abstraction.

As far as cubism as a sculptural form is concerned, Jacques Lipchitz, who is of Polish extraction, may be said to be the artist who has best realized its possibilities. And he, too, has made a liberal use of the hollowed-out surface, though his method of handling planes is quite different from that employed by Archipenko or Zadkine, and is in fact more closely allied to that used by the painters, so much so that at times the work appears to be conceived as a two-, instead of as a three-dimensional, form. Incidentally, also his *Reclining Woman with a Guitar* is one of the typically pictorial subjects of the period, as are other of his compositions, yet in translating it into terms of stone, he has done so in a singularly consistent way, while there is considerable subtlety in the transition from the concave to the convex form, which he has achieved in one sweep from the head to the forearm. It will be observed, also, that the perforations of the block (the method which corresponds to Moholy-Nagy's third stage in the evolution of sculpture) are an integral part of the work as a whole. In addition, the placing of the guitar at the focal point gives a strength, like the key-stone of a building, that is needed both to stabilize the design and to introduce the necessary contrast of a rectangular form.

But perhaps the most brilliant applications of a form of facet cubism to sculpture is that exemplified in Picasso's *Bronze Head* of 1909, which is of the same date as his landscape *Factory at Horta de Ebro*, the first painting to which the term cubist was applied. And it is characteristic of the great Spaniard that he should have produced, in what for him was a novel medium, a work that is not only one of unusual energy and power, but one that is also completely coherent by sculptural standards. His own *Portrait* by his fellow-countryman Paul Gargallo, on the other hand, which is in the Barcelona

[1] *The Meaning of Modern Sculpture* by R. H. Wilenski. Faber & Faber. London, 1932.

Museum, though equally vigorous and though carved with commendable economy, produces an effect that is more aggressive than forceful, simply because a momentary pose is rendered with a definition that is final and allows therefore of no implied relaxation. It is, moreover, a work in complete contrast to Gargallo's usual manner, which is elegant in the extreme, though it is characteristic of the outstanding originality of his approach. For it is in the development of the art of metal sculpture that Gargallo has excelled, his *Urano* being a typical example of his style in this medium, which for all its extraordinarily decorative quality goes beyond the merely ornamental in the strength of its evocative and imaginative power and its essential lyricism.

Another Spanish sculptor of the modern school who has devoted himself to experimental work in metal is Julio Gonzalez, who has lived and worked mainly in Paris. His work, however, is of an entirely different kind and is altogether less poetic in inspiration, as is evident in his construction of a *Woman Arranging her Hair*, which anyone might be supported in thinking to be arbitrarily so named. For there is a great deal to be said in favour of the argument that much unnecessary prejudice is aroused by the persistent habit among artists of the abstract school of retaining representational titles for their unrepresentational subjects, the interest of which centres in something entirely different. Indeed, considering the prejudices of the artists themselves (for of all prejudiced people, save of course the critics, artists are the most so), there would seem to be something almost unethical in the practice. This, however, in no way affects the structural qualities of the work, though one may hesitate to accept George L. K. Morris's view that Gonzalez was endowed 'with an unparalleled facility in the handling of metals', a medium, as he goes on to say, that he has been free to carry to 'its expressive limits'.

Such an artist as José Clará, who is commonly accepted as the leading master of the orthodox school in Spain, would not recognize the wholly non-plastic work of the constructivist school as sculpture at all, while the exponents of the modern movements might be equally justified in asking what precisely a neo-classical bronze of the type of Clará's *Eve* contributes to the enrichment of human experience, despite its obvious sculptural qualities. Indeed, like the wearied *maître de ballet*, who after eighteen auditions stipulated that the rest of the dancers must choose something instead of Fokine's Swan Dance if they expected to be considered, even the most unprejudiced critic might be forgiven for pleading for something else instead of another Eve. Thus, while on the one hand Spain has produced artists who are among the most advanced of the century, she has, on the other, nurtured a number of sculptors, like José Clará, Mateo Inurria, Enric Casanovas and Josep Capuz, who have adhered with exceptional fidelity to the traditional styles of the academies.

Sweden is a land of many sculptors of whom Carl Milles and Ivar Johnsson are by far the most distinguished, though by accepted standards, Christian Eriksson, Carl Eldh, John Lundqvist, Eric Grate and Bror Hjorth are also sculptors of eminence whose work might be discussed in a more comprehensive survey.

Carl Milles is, however, unique, being one of the very few artists who have succeeded in introducing humour into sculpture and of doing so with a verve that is uniformly sustained. It is significant, also, that his sense of style is most conspicuously exhibited in those examples of his work in which he has had the opportunity to indulge this particular aspect of his genius, whether it be in forms that are sardonic, witty or merely bland, in all of which the ends are achieved with equal conviction. Hence, it is upon such a work as his inimitable *Folke Filbyter*, which represents the grandfather of the founder of the Folkung dynasty on his legendary journey through Sweden in search of his grandson, that the signs of his originality as a sculptor are most forcibly impressed. This work, which, like most of Milles' sculpture, is in bronze, is the central figure of the Folk Filbyter Fountain in Stockholm and is one of several fountains which vary from the *Poseidon Fountain*, another mannered and highly successful composition, to the *Triton Fountain*, in which his choice of motifs is less felicitous. For it would be difficult to imagine figures either less impressive in themselves or less impressively grouped than those two-tailed mermen which are only a degree less meaningless by expression than his female fountain figures of similar type. His beautiful *Sun Singer*, which he executed as a memorial to a poet, reveals however the clarity of style of which he is capable when engaged on a subject that evokes a lyrical response.

Among other notable achievements Milles has executed the *Four Ages of Exchange* in black granite for the Enskilda Bank in Stockholm and the statue of *Rudbeckius* at Västeras, Sweden, both works in a satiric vein, while in America, where he took up his residence in 1932 as a professor of sculpture at the Cranbrook Academy in Michigan, he has produced the *Harrisburg Doors* and the *Peace Monument* for the City Hall, which is carved in Mexican onyx and is representative of an entirely new style in which the influence of indigenous American art is evident. Whether his removal to America is likely to prove to his ultimate advantage as an artist must remain, however, a matter of conjecture, but even if it were not to do so, Milles would still be ranked among the most original sculptors of his generation.

Ivar Johnsson, who may be taken as the other representative of modern Swedish sculpture, is an artist whose gifts are of an entirely different order. Having studied in Italy he was at one time strongly influenced by the art of the Renaissance and by classical prototypes, but on his return to Sweden he later developed a realistic style of his own, which, for all its intensity, is marked by a sense of control that serves, paradoxically enough, only to increase its emotional power. Thus, in his *Fugitive Woman*, he makes no attempt to elaborate this theme, but by the very directness of his method contrives to emphasize the urgency of her flight. Similarly, there is something so essentially honest in his handling of the *Man in the Shetland Jersey* and of his *Woman by the Sea* that they gain thereby a quality of nobility that, on the face of it, they would hardly be expected to exhibit. But of all his work, which includes both architectural and fountain sculpture, his commemorative statue to *Tycho Brahe*, the Danish astronomer, is the most memorable.

In Switzerland, as in Spain, sculptors are sharply divided into two schools—those who remain more or less content with conventional modes, and those who have turned from figurative to non-figurative forms of artistic expression.

Of the first group Hermann Haller is probably the best known, for although he has been described as wholeheartedly modern, he is modern only in respect of the greater freedom of his technique, which, considering the ordinary nature of his ideas, cannot, on the whole, be regarded as an improvement, since it is doubtful whether the roughness of his finish adds very much to the not very pungent character of his nudes, just as it is questionable whether his equestrian statue to *Hans Waldemann* gains anything from those modifications of a traditional style that he has introduced. Two other sculptors who belong to this group are Herman Hubacher, who has worked mainly as a *busteur*, and Carl Burckhardt, whose work varies from his *Eve*, which is slightly reminiscent of the polychromatic statuary of the German sculptor Max Klinger, to his *Dancer*, which is more nearly akin to the dancers of Ernesto di Fiori, for like so many sculptors of the period, he, too, was attracted to the dance as a sculptural theme.

The second group is represented by Alberto Giacometti and Max Bill. The art of the first is abstract with a surrealist bias, while that of the second is mainly constructivist in character.

In some ways, Giacometti is the most human and the most charming of abstract artists, for although his work is fundamentally serious in the best sense, there is a touch of fantasy about it that renders even those of his carvings which are comparatively slight in conception entirely delightful. So that, when he entitles a quadrilateral block with two hollows, two flutings and three incised lines, *Personnage*, it is quite obvious that the sculpture is an entity and that that is its name. Similarly, there is a quality that may justly be termed exquisite about those of his carvings that are more purely abstract, the apparent severity of the form of such a work as his faceted plaster *Sculpture 1933-34* being insufficient to obscure the intrinsic originality of Giacometti's sculptural approach.

Max Bill, on the other hand, is more consciously occupied, like the Russian constructivists, with the exploration of the laws which govern spatial relationships and his work is consequently less imaginative and more severely architectonic in character. But experiments in the balancing of forms as in his metal *Constructions in Equal Elements*, with which he was concerned shortly before the war, do not exhaust either his interest or his resources, since he has produced a number of works that are plastic rather than constructive in character, the latest of these being his giant *Continuity*, which had recently been erected in Zurich. In reproduction, it seems doubtful whether the interest of the form is adequate to the scale on which the idea is carried out, but until one has seen the work *in situ* it would be invidious to dogmatize, just as it would be unwise, on the basis of what has already been accomplished, to hazard an opinion as to the probable development of the art of sculpture during the second half of the present century.

INDEX OF SCULPTORS

THE PLATES

I

ERIC GILL: Crucifixion, 1910

ERIC GILL: Flying Angel. C.1928

2

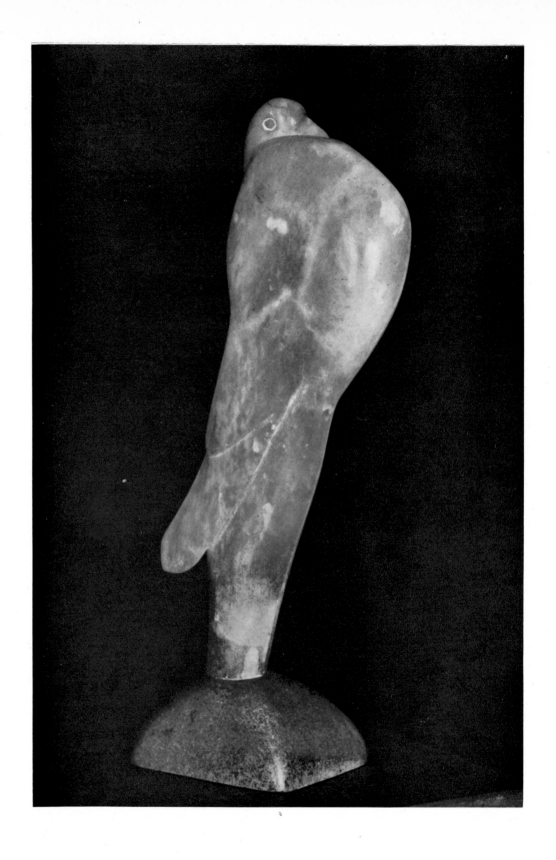

3   JOHN SKEAPING: Pouter Pigeon. C. 1933

RICHARD BEDFORD: Opening Bud. 1940

4

5   JACOB EPSTEIN: Rabindranath Tagore. 1927

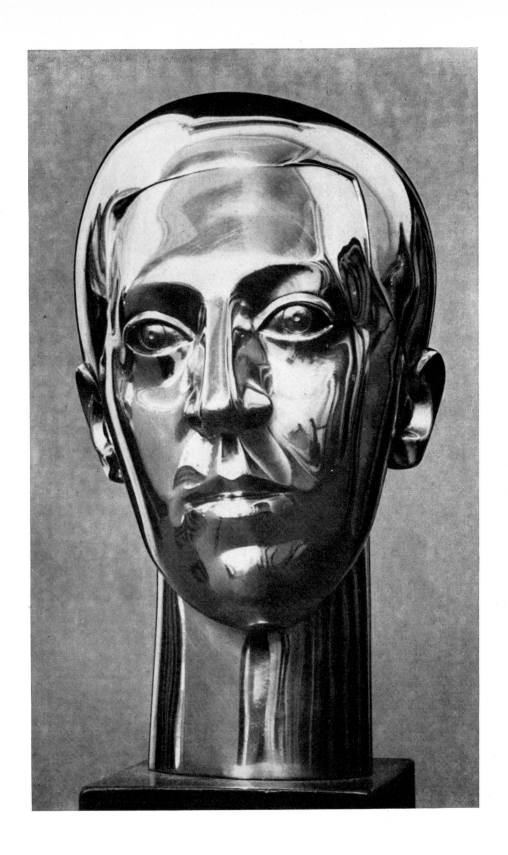

FRANK DOBSON: Sir Osbert Sitwell. 1923

6

7   HENRY MOORE: Mother and Child. 1931

HENRY MOORE: Reclining Figure. 1940   8

9   BARBARA HEPWORTH: Pierced Hemisphere. 1937

BARBARA HEPWORTH: Elegy. 1946   IO

II ROBERT ADAMS: Seated Woman. 1947

F. E. MCWILLIAM: Reclining Woman. 1947

12

13   DORA GORDINE: Chinese Philosopher. 1927

GEORGE MINNE: Relic Bearer. 1929   14

15   RIK WOUTERS: Bust of the Sculptor

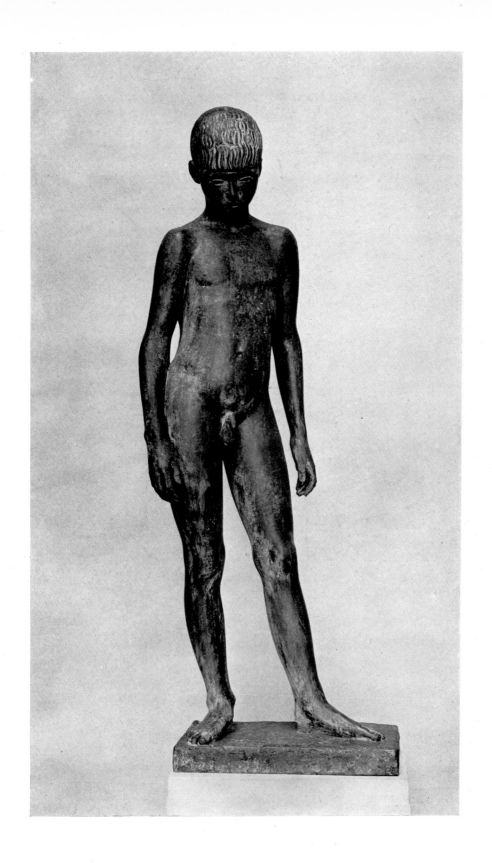

CHARLES LEPLAE: Luco

16

17   JAN STURSA: Bust of the Sculptor's Mother. 1921

JAN STURSA: Falling Warrior. 1921   18

19   JAN LAUDA: Head of an Old Man

YRJO LIIPOLA: Awakening Strength. 1911　　　20

21   WAINO AALTONEN: Sibelius. 1936

WAINO AALTONEN: Paavo Nurmi. 1927   22

23   EMIL HALONEN: Girl. 1908

JOHANNES HAAPSALO: Archer. 1926

24

25   AUGUSTE RODIN: Hand of God. 1898

AUGUSTE RODIN: Prodigal Son

26

27   ARISTIDE MAILLOL: Three Nymphs

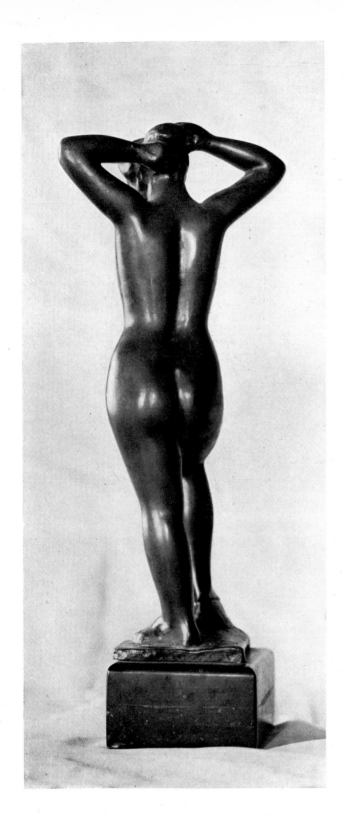

ARISTIDE MAILLOL: Woman Dressing her Hair (two views)   28

29   CHARLES DESPIAU: Paulette. 1907

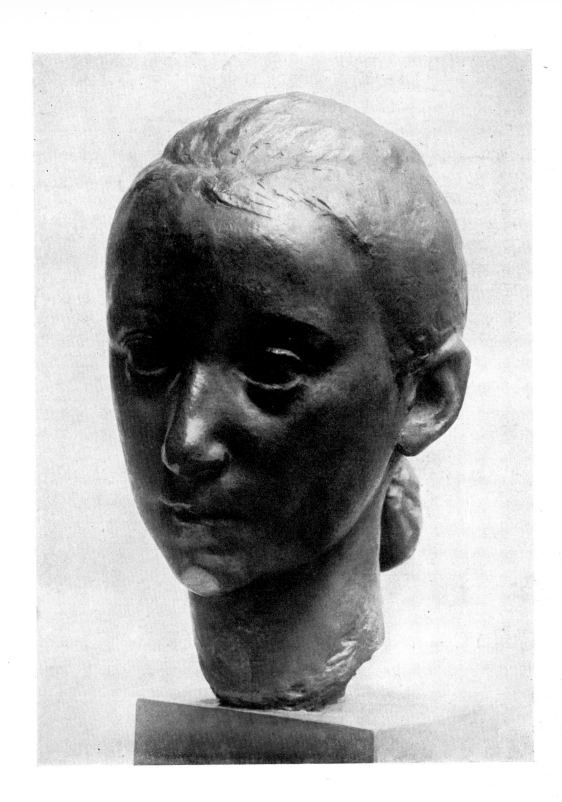

CHARLES DESPIAU: Petite Fille des Landes. 1904   30

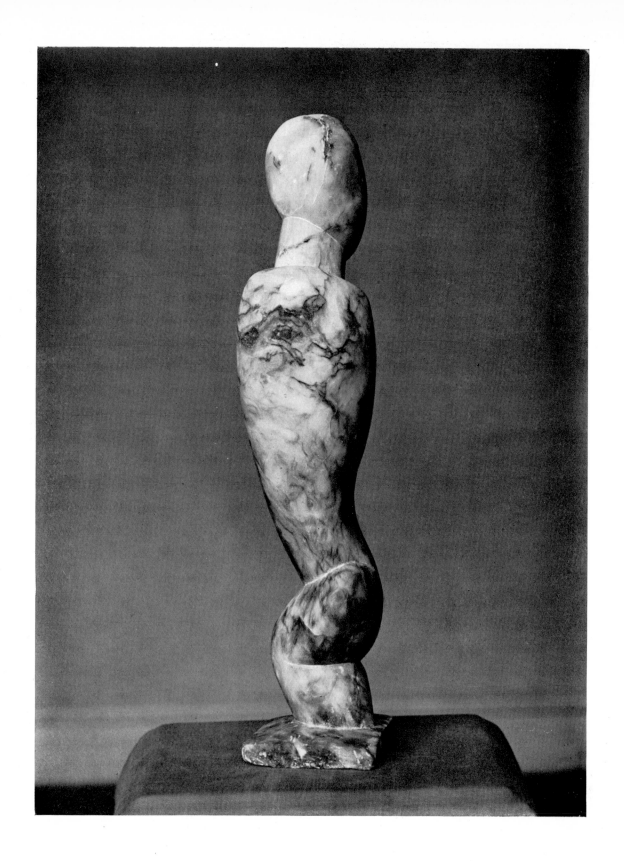

31   HENRI GAUDIER-BRZESKA: The Imp. C.1912

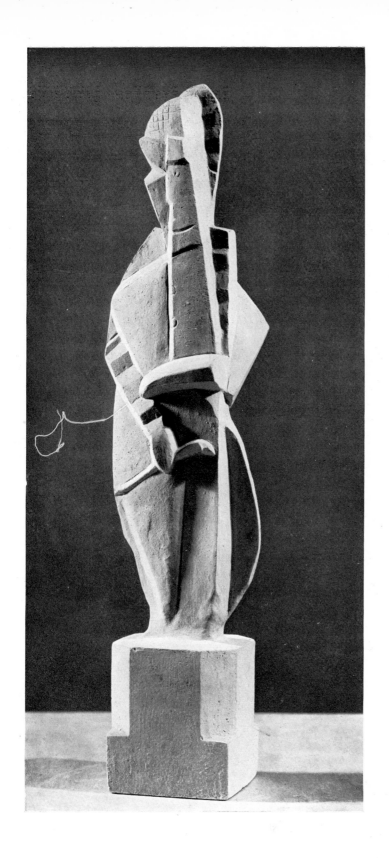

HENRI LAURENS: Jockey. 1921

32

33   JEAN ARP: Sculpture Méditerrannéenne. 1941

JEAN ARP and SOPHIE TAUBER-ARP: Sculpture Conjugale. 1937   34

35   GEORG KOLBE: Young Man Stepping Forward (detail). 1928

GEORG KOLBE: Genius of Beethoven (detail). 1926   36

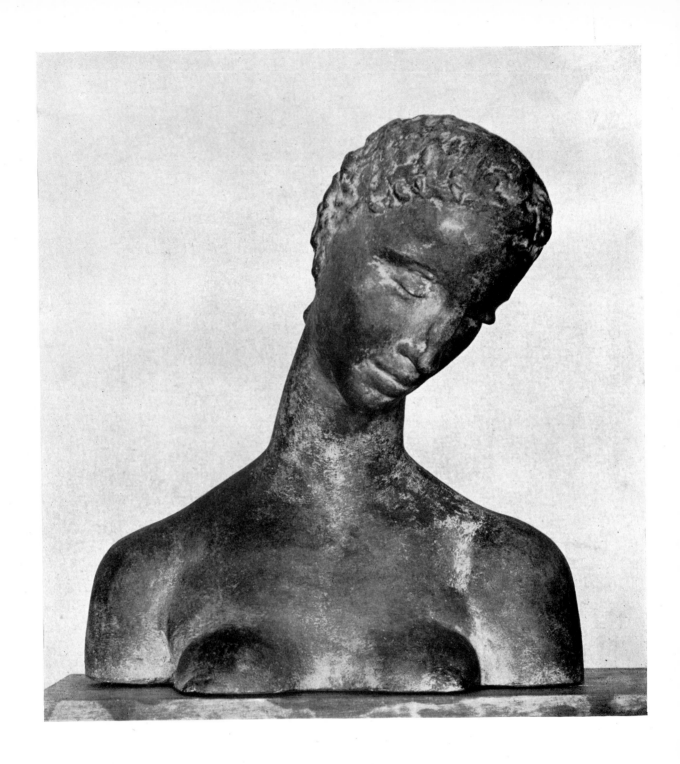

37   WILHELM LEHMBRUCK: Bust

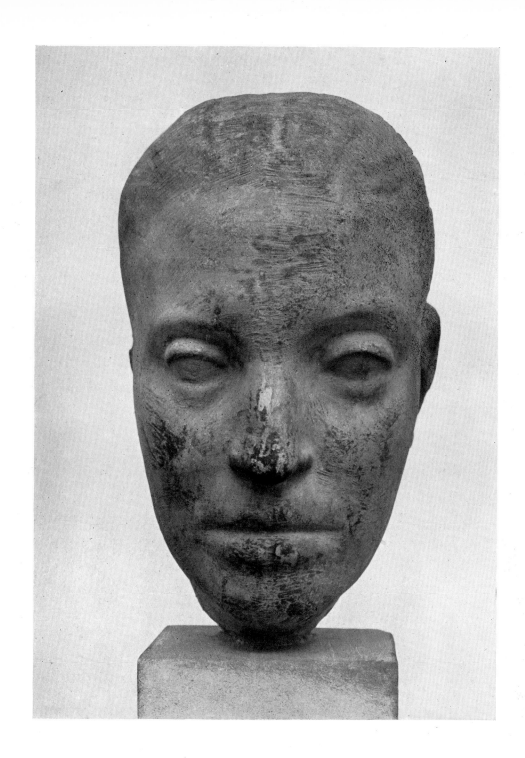

WILHELM LEHMBRUCK: Head

38

39   ERNST BARLACH: Panic-stricken. 1912

ERNST BARLACH: The Avenger. 1923

41   GERHARDT MARCKS: Girl with Apple. 1936

HILDO KROP: Female Figure

42

43   LAJOS VAN EBNETH: Head of a Man. 1946

JOHN RADECKER: Head of a Man   44

45   MARINO MARINI: Mme Hedy Hahnloser-Buhler. 1944

ALBERTO VIANI: Torso. 1945

46

47   IVAN MESTROVIC: Torso: Strahanić Ban

IVAN MESTROVIC: Lute Player

48

49   EMIL LIE: Seated Boy. 1933

GUSTAV VIGELAND: Henrik Wergeland. 1907

50

51   CONSTANTIN BRANCUSI: Torso of a Young Girl. 1922

CONSTANTIN BRANCUSI: The New Born. 1920   52

53   ALEXANDER ARCHIPENKO: Standing Figure. 1942

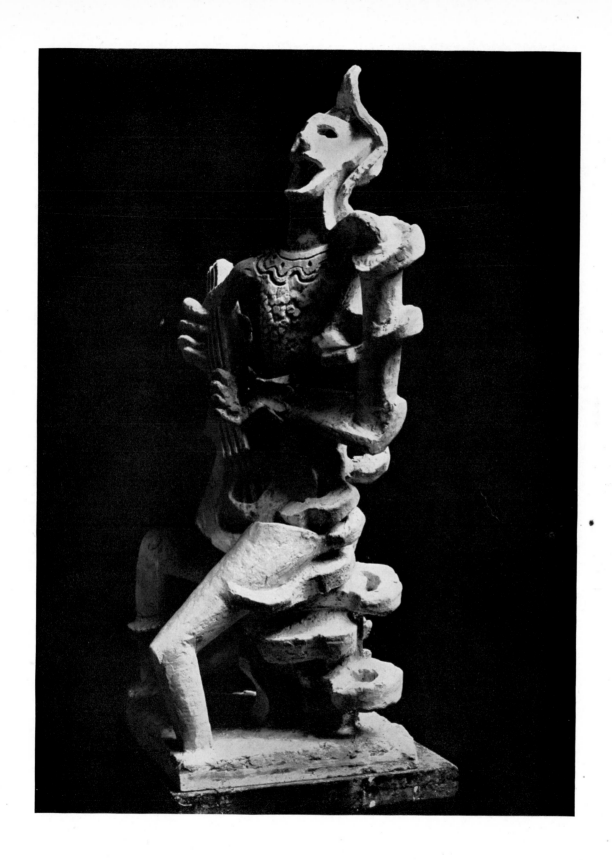

OSIP ZADKINE: Harlequin. 1933   **54**

55   JACQUES LIPCHITZ: Reclining Woman with a Guitar. 1928

PAU GARGALLO: Urano. 1933

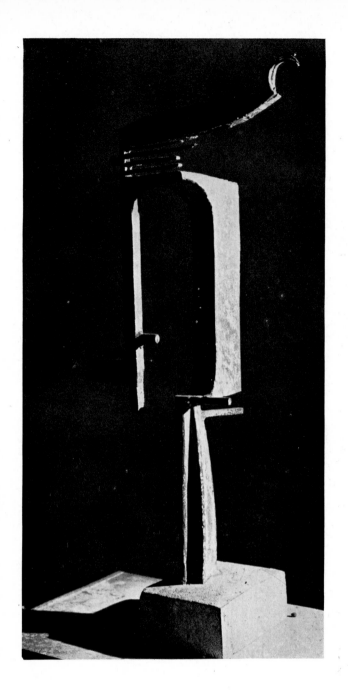

57A

JULIO GONZALEZ: Woman Arranging her Hair

MATEO INURRIA: Flower of Granada

57B

JOSE CLARA: Eve. 1938

58

59

PABLO PICASSO: Head. 1909

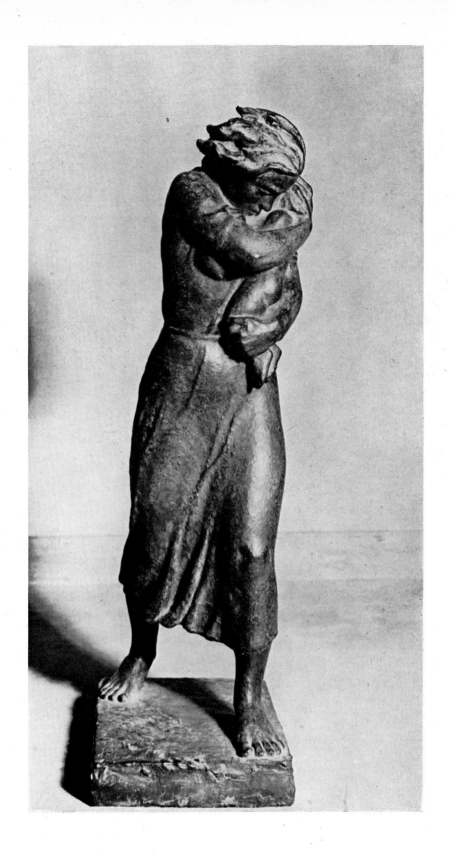

IVAR JOHNSSON: Fugitive Woman. 1935   60

61.   CARL MILLES: Folke Filbyter. 1927

CARL MILLES: Sun Singer. 1926

63   MAX BILL: Continuity. 1947